SCENES FROM THE PAST : 26 (PART THREE)

JOURNEYS BY EXCURSION TRAIN FROM

- EAST LANCASHI

PREST

via KIRKHAM and the MARTON LINE

to

BLACKPOOL

(CENTRAL)

STUART TAYLOR

ISBN 1 870119 51 7

Designed by Stuart Taylor

Printed by
Amadeus Press
Cleckheaton

Published by
Foxline
(Publications)
Limited
PO Box 84
Bredbury.
SK6 3YD

Acknowledgements

My sincere thanks to those persons and organisations listed below for without their help, this "outing" to Blackpool Central simply would not have been possible. Special thanks must go to Peter Fitton. His enthusiasm for these excursion books has kept me going during the last few years; thanks Peter, and thank you all for your time and efforts. *AerofilmsLtd., Arnold Battson, Blackpool Corporation Department of Tourism, Blackpool Evening Gazette, Tony Bretherton, A. H. Bryant, Gordon Coltas, Jim Davenport, "Young" Jim Dean, Frank Dean's pictures and Diaries loaned by Jim Markland and Brian Pickersgill (photos) with acknowledgement to Carl England, John Fozard, Dorron Harper, R. B. Holden, Frank Hornby, Hulton Getty Picture Collection Ltd., Denis Keenan, Tom Lewis, G. H. Platt, John E. Porter, Rail Archive Stephenson, Raleigh Industries. Special thanks to Brian Randle and Ernie Allen for details of Raleigh Industries at Nottingham, Geoff Robinson, Don Rutter, Tothill Press, Mike Bentley, for the Harry Townley photos, and Graham Whitehead.*

As always I must pay tribute to my family for their help in the preparation of this volume, to Gemma (George Formby details), Robert and Richard for computer work and Barbara.........Thank you one and and all..***Stuart Taylor***

Having a refresher (title page). This view shows a mixture of drivers passed men and guards, all having a day out looking over the road into Blackpool Central in readiness for working the season's specials. These days out would be just prior to Easter, and would involve men from a great many depots and a number of regional areas. This particular picture was taken in the spring of 1954 on number 10 (excursion) platform at Blackpool Central. *Hulton Getty Picture Collection Ltd.*

Beneath the Tower. We had constantly watched the "Old vinegar bottle" getting bigger since our first sighting of it by bridge 102 on the Marton Line, and by the time we finally drew into the Central station, Blackpool's 518 foot tower seemed colossal to say the least. Invariably it was decked in scaffolding at some point and we would always watch open mouthed as the spidermen clambered around the steelwork applying the "red lead" coating. This **July 1962** view shows the Central station platforms 4, 5 and 6 in the foreground and platform 7 of the excursion side, just to the right of the old steam heat boilers. *G. H. Platt*

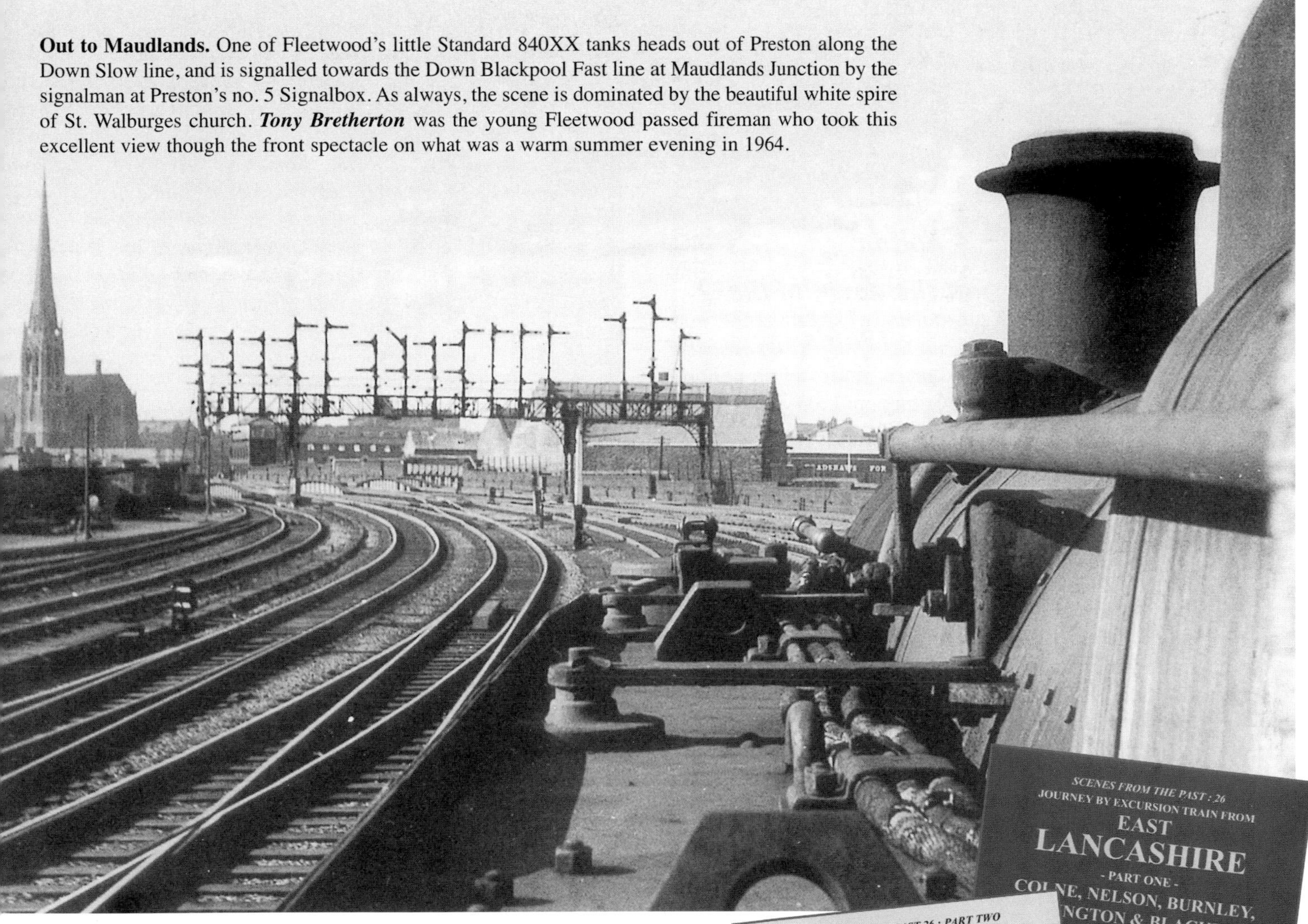

Out to Maudlands. One of Fleetwood's little Standard 840XX tanks heads out of Preston along the Down Slow line, and is signalled towards the Down Blackpool Fast line at Maudlands Junction by the signalman at Preston's no. 5 Signalbox. As always, the scene is dominated by the beautiful white spire of St. Walburges church. ***Tony Bretherton*** was the young Fleetwood passed fireman who took this excellent view though the front spectacle on what was a warm summer evening in 1964.

Contents

Introduction...4 - 7

Starting Point..8 - 9

Farington Curve Junction

to Preston Station.....................................10 - 27

Fishergate Bridge

to Fylde Junction.......................................28 - 35

Fylde Junction

to Kirkham North Junction....................36 - 59

Bradkirk to Blackpool Central.................60 - 109

Along the Central Promenade................110 - 123

Blackpool Illuminations..........................124 - 127

Other FOXLINE titles by STUART TAYLOR

Those changing years 1959 - 63

The "lad" himself
Stuart Taylor
A holiday moment
at the dawn of the
1960's

Introduction.

At long last we're off to Blackpool. My apologies to those of you who have been patiently waiting for these Blackpool books. Four years have passed since my first book *The Railways of Colne* was prepared. Believe it or not, this whole excursion series we are now involved with was originally designed to be just an eight page feature article within that same "Colne" book. Whilst the idea of the Colne book itself came from working with Eric Laycock, a brilliant railwayman and a good workmate, the true idea behind the excursion series relates to a slightly earlier period, January 1992. We had just lost Dad, and one night as I sifted through the paperwork associated with those sad events, my ears pricked as over in the lounge I could hear the sound of Ben E. King singing his memorable 1961 hit "Stand by me". It was the start of a film which bore the same name, a film about the events in some youn American kid's lives. In no time at all I had drifted back in m mind to those happy days as the 1950's ended and the 'sixtie took off, that time in life when you start to show a serious interes in your parents, trying to understand their world as well as you own. It was also the time when those happy outings by rail to th Lancashire Coast seemed to be changing, our decade of travel b steam train to Blackpool, etc. was almost over. It was as the soun of Ben E. King faded away that I became very aware that the bes part of thirty years had passed since those happy outings ha ended, and clearly something had to done to record those events Thanks to Greg Fox this has been possible, and I quickly foun that Greg and myself were very much on the same wavelength, fo once, here was a publisher you could work seriously with, person with a creative mind to match my own. Parts three an four of volume twenty six therefore will relate to the railways t and from the Fylde coast.

This third part then, covers the journey from Preston to Blackpoo Central, travelling over the Marton line from Kirkham to Black pool South. We feature the Central station in detail together wit a look at the Central promenade and those "stars of stage an television" who entertained us so well in the summers' of th 1950's and 60's.

Seaside memories. Sifting through my spotting books, up popped **46147** in an old "Woolies" red jotter dating from 1958. The summer, it will be recalled, was warm and sunny, the winter however, will always be remembered for the snowy conditions which caused the fatal aircrash at Munich involving Manchester United Football Club, the "Busby Babes". Near the front of that little red notepad were details relating to the legendary young soccer player Duncan Edwards. The entry relating to **46147**, *The Northamptonshire Regiment* appeared later amongst the summer spottings at Blackpool. The engine would be one of the 29 "Scots" withdrawn at the end of the 1962 summer timetable. *A.H.Bryant*

Home sweet home. No. 6 Greenwood Terrace, the third house on the right, was our home throughout those excursion years. We'd often dash the quarter of a mile or so to the station in the local holidays to catch our half day excursion for the coast. Dad's hen pens are in the right foreground. What would we have done without those egg "butties" on our excursion outings? *S.Taylor.*

Part four will be entitled "Return from Blackpool Central", and as the title infers, will see us making a return journey from Blackpool Central, the idea being to recreate the atmosphere of the journey home to East Lancashire the way it was on those balmy summer evenings during our excursion years. The return trip will include a detailed look at the "Coast" line through Squires Gate, St. Annes, Ansdell and Fairhaven, and Lytham as well as the rural stations at Moss Side and Wrea Green. Featured areas on the return journey include Preston, Blackburn, Accrington, the Great Harwood - Padiham loop line and Rose Grove. Views are included all the way back to Colne, where our excursion series began in part one. However, before we take that journey back home we will be doing a bit of serious "train spotting" down at the locomotive sheds at Blackpool, looking in some detail at the men and machines of the steam era. Footplatemen from Blackpool, Rose Grove, and even Bradford's Low Moor depot will be seen. A feature article looks at how these "Lanky" men from Low Moor came to work the "Jazzer" K 3's down the Calder Valley and though East Lancashire to Blackpool in the summers' up to 1962. The routes from Kirkham to Blackpool North and Fleetwood will be dealt with in another book, but more of that later.

As you may be aware, these books relate to my own personal experiences, my memories of the way things were back the 1950's etc. In effect, it's a look at how my family spent the annual holidays in July each year from 1952 to 1963. As this series of books has evolved, I have tried to give a personal insight into what was happening in our lives at the time and how we accepted the changes brought about as part of the growing up process, as well as those imposed upon us in what was a markedly changing world in that period from the late 1950's into the early 1960's. From an era of tradition and austerity in post war Britain, youngsters such as ourselves who became teenagers with the coming of the 1960's sometimes found it hard to come to terms with the modern world. Too many things seemed to alter all at once as the 1950's drew to a close. The changes which occurred on the railway as part of the Beeching era would be particulary hard to accept. The heading title of the introduction, "Those changing years 1959 - 62", really relates to the next part of the text. It is a personal thought, but I have long been of the impression that the events surrounding the coming of television into most of our homes had a profound effect on our lives from that period on. Throughout the 1950's our knowledge of what was happening in the world, be it fashion, music, holidays, etc; all came via the newspapers, the odd magazine, the cinema, and the radio. Television was the turning point in all our lives, a whole new world suddenly opening up for us. Post-war Britain seemed to be slumbering through the 1950's, but all that changed with the coming of television. Rental TV took off in a big way during the priod 1959 - 60. For example, a 17inch black and white set would cost around nine "bob" a week, and so affordable it seems was the new medium, that in no time at all, what had been a trickle of new viewers in the late 50's, turned into a torrent of "telly addicts" by the early 1960's. We warmed to the likes of Hughie Green, Michael Miles, Eamonn Andrews; we laughed at situation comedies such as "The Army Game", and "The Larkins" with David Kossoff and the bellowing Peggy Mount. We thrilled at the "cowboy" series such as "Rawhide", "Wagon Train", "Bonanza" and "Laramie", and we longed to visit those far off climates seen in the travel shows or visited by the likes of Alan Wicker. Once we had seen a few sundrenched foreign beaches it was hard to look at a day trip to Blackpool in the same light. Our little terraced home bought by rental purchase for a mere £400 back in the 1950's had no hot water except for the coal fired back boiler. It had an outside toilet and the bath hung on a nail in the yard. But when television came on the scene, we were amongst the first in the row to have one. In no time at all, the trusty Ewbank carpet sweeper had been replaced by a electric cylinder vacuum; a twin tub washer had appeared, and by 1962 there was even talk of a fridge!.... By late 1960, when for example, "Coronation Street" began its seemingly endless run on the "telly", we were casting away old traditions at an alarming rate. One of those traditions, the cinema, was suffering particulary badly, the television stations having bought the rights to many of the feature films of the 1940's and 50's.. ***Continued on page 7***

ECS at Colne. Rose Grove driver Jock Morrison brings "Grove's" **44940** into Colne tender first with a set of coaches for a Blackpool working in the summer of 1961. Fireman Joe Carroll jumps off to brew, whilst his mate runs round the stock. *Young Jim Dean.*

Those changing years 1959 - 63

Where were you in '62? Joe Brown, the boy next door with the cheeky grin, was no. 1 in the charts as we began our last year of normal day trips on the "Runabout Rover" tickets from Colne to the Lancashire Coast in July 1962. His trade marks were the spiky "hairdo" and the big Gibson 335 guitar, with its shoulder strap full of horse brasses. Ex-Plaistow fireman Joe had left the railway when redundancy loomed on the LT & S line in London's East End. By 1960, instead of shovelling coal on the line to Southend, he was touring with such rock legends as Gene Vincent and Eddie Cochran. **(above)** Bert, Dad and Mum at Blackpool and **45681** *Aboukir* at Colne carriage sidings, with Bonny Colne upon the hill in the background. *Tothill Press, Brian Wrigglesworth and Stuart Taylor.*

7 July 1962

Last week	This week	Title / Artist (Label)
2	1	A PICTURE OF YOU — Joe Brown (Piccadilly)
4	2	I CAN'T STOP LOVING YOU — Ray Charles (HMV)
1	3	COME OUTSIDE — Mike Sarne (Parlophone)
3	4	GOOD LUCK CHARM — Elvis Presley (RCA)
5	5	GINNY COME LATELY — Brian Hyland (HMV)
6	6	I'M LOOKING OUT THE WINDOW — Cliff Richard (Columbia)
9	7	HERE COMES THAT FEELING — Brenda Lee (Brunswick)
10	8	THE GREEN LEAVES OF SUMMER — Kenny Ball & His Jazzmen (Pye Jazz)
7	9	LAST NIGHT WAS MADE FOR LOVE — Billy Fury (Decca)
16	10	ENGLISH COUNTRY GARDEN — Jimmie Rodgers (Columbia)
16	11	FOLLOW THAT DREAM (EP) — Elvis Presley (RCA)
13	12	STRANGER ON THE SHORE — Mr Acker Bilk (Columbia)
12	13	AIN'T THAT FUNNY — Jimmy Justice (Pye)
8	14	I DON'T KNOW WHY — Eden Kane (Decca)
14	15	AS YOU LIKE IT — Adam Faith (Parlophone)
18	16	YES, MY DARLING DAUGHTER — Eydie Gorme (CBS)
20	17	SHARING YOU — Bobby Vee (Liberty)

Continued from page 5...... Our local Savoy closed its doors in the July of 1960 to become a "Scotts Supermarket", something which we considered to be highly American at the time. Of the range of new gadgets that came with that modern era at the end of the 1950's, I think the new record player, a Dansette Conquest Auto was probably favourite. It sounded great - and still does! We would often stack up the likes of Bobby Vee, Helen Shapiro and The Drifters with Ben E. King, on the 45 r.p.m. deck of the old Dansette. Marty Wilde and Cliff and the Shadows were equally favourite at the time and I do vividly remember imitating that famous "Shadows" walk as we listened to records like FBI. Now while all the social niceties of this new modern way of life were becoming apparent, traditional things in our lives such as the annual train trips to the seaside seemed to continue just the way they had done since the start of the 1950's. Each year the excursion handbills would appear just the way they had the year before, only the date being altered, and that's the way it stayed until the summer of 1962. By that time the railways were deeply in debt and yet ticket prices rose only by sixpence or a shilling a year. Clearly something had to give......and it did. The year of 1962 would be the last normal year of excursion travel as we had known it. In that summer we would encounter our first difficulty in ten years of rail travel on the excursions. In the course of our July 1962 run about trips we noticed that the stations at Fleetwood and Morecambe Euston Road seemed decidedly quiet compared with other years. Blackpool Central meanwhile was its usual busy self with lots of special trains and literally thousands of day-trippers entering the resort via its fourteen platforms, giving little hint of the fate which awaited it some two years later.

Bashful Bob. The multi talented American singer Bobby Vee, who serenaded us during those fading excursion years, also felt the wind of change as the era of Beatlemania took off in the summer of 1963.
Tothill Press.

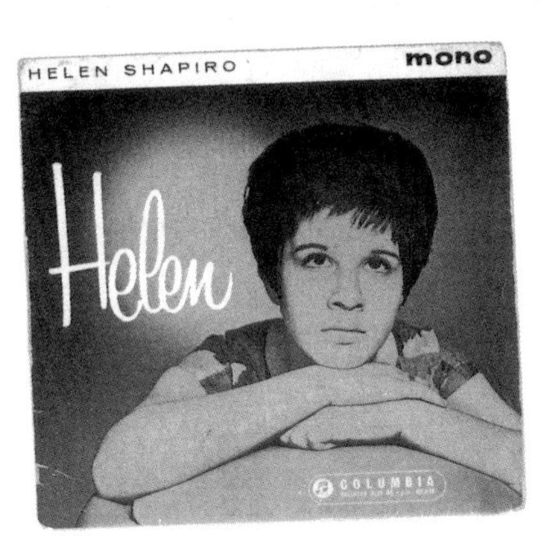

In that 1962-63 period we were mere teenagers enjoying the usual experiences of growing up and were therefore oblivious as to the implications of the Beeching report and how it would affect our future summer outings by rail. As the Beeching plan was unveiled in March 1963, we were busily dating girls, more often than not occupying the back row seats of the local Hippodrome cinema watching such films as "633 Squadron", Elvis's "Girls, Girls, Girls" and "Follow that dream"; Also James Bond in "From Russia with Love", and the pop classic "Just for fun", which starred Mark Wynter, Joe Brown, Jet Harris and Tony Meehan, and not forgetting of course Bobby Vee and Johnny Tillotson. When we think back to that time in 1963 and recall just how much we were unaware of what the Beeching proposals actually meant in terms of our future rail travel, it makes you realise that maybe we weren't the only ones who were unaware of events that were taking place around them. Take the likes of teenage idol Bobby Vee as a prime example. He may well have been somewhat innocent as to the impending changes that were to take place in the world of pop music during that summer of 1963. At the time, Bobby was riding high in the charts with "The night has a thousand eyes", and it is possible that this now classic record was really the swansong at the end of yet another era, for as we all know, the Beatles, those nasal sounding Liverpudlians with their brash young sound, had arrived on the scene. They were very much idolised by my girlfriend of the time, the lovely Lorraine Cummings (her of the sexy eyelashes and freckles) and in the summer of 1963 they would literally take the country by storm. It was they above all who seemed to epitomise that modern new world that so many of us were just not ready for. As far as I'm concerned, the Beatles will always be associated with that era of change in the early 1960's, the time when our happy summer outings by rail to the Lancashire coast sadly came to an end. I have to admit though, that I did come to terms with that new world of the sixties quite quickly and I even bought the Beatles first LP at Southport in July of 1963, but only because they did a fine rendition of the Hal David/Burt Bacharach song "Baby its you", that had already been a hit for the Shirelles. So there you have just a little bit of an insight as to how we felt at the onset of the 1960's. Time now to head for Blackpool.

Stuart Taylor,
Colne, Lancashire.
July 1997

Departures from Preston. *The Kings Regiment Liverpool* **46132**, stands at the head of the 11.29a.m. to Workington on Saturday 22nd June 1963. That final excursion summer was glorious and as always at Preston, the air seemed fresher and the light somewhat brighter than back home in East Lancashire. Across on page 9 we see my good friend and Blackpool engineman, Don Rutter, standing on the tender fall plate of 5X **45584** *North West Frontier*. With him is driver Alf Chew; they are working the 5.15p.m. Manchester - Blackpool Central slow passenger train on Friday 17th August 1962. Note how the rear driving wheels need re-profiling. *Ray Farrell and Peter Fitton.*

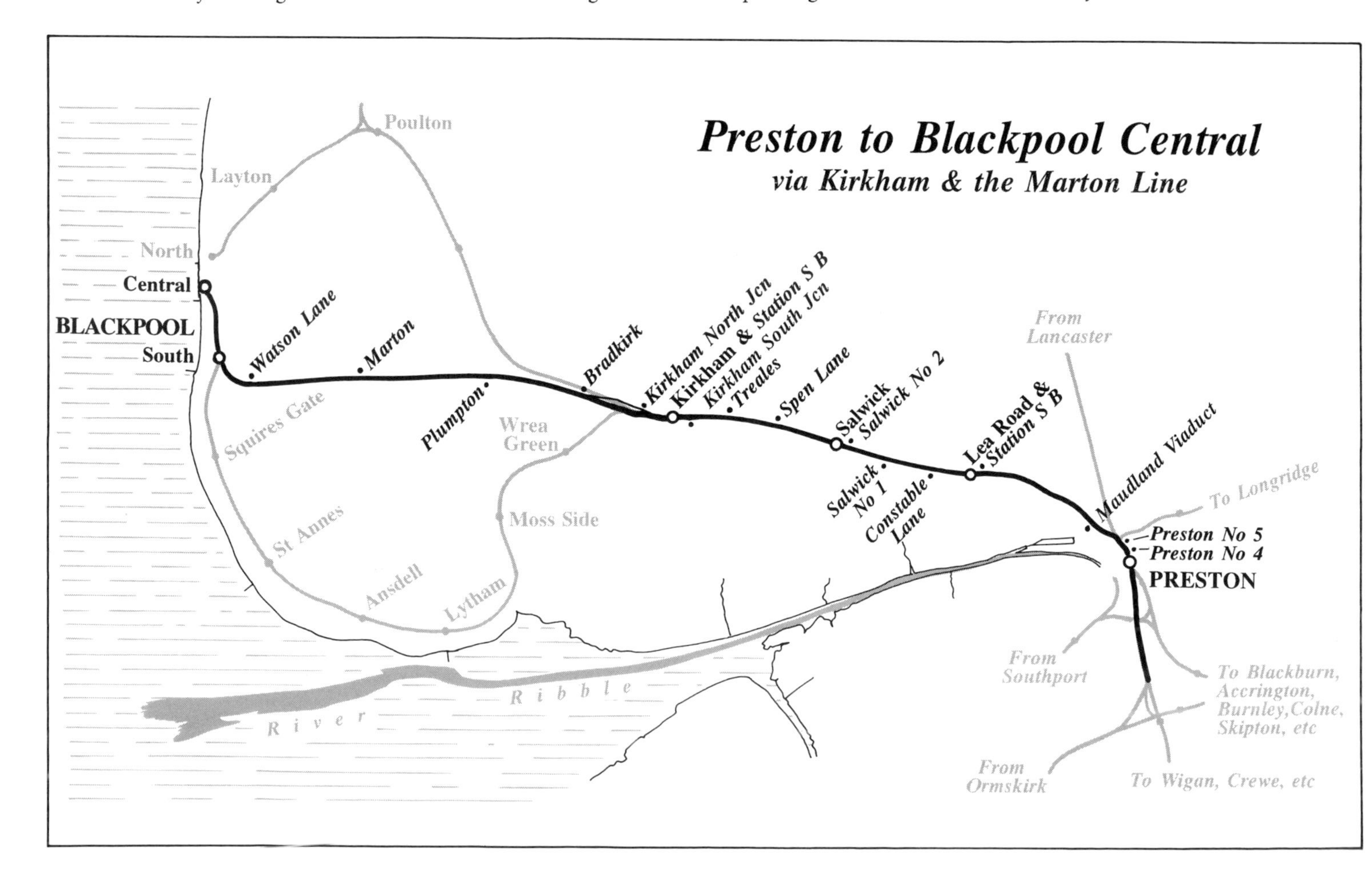

Preston Fylde Junction to Blackpool via the Marton Line.

Very occasionally on the Blackpool runs we would travel from Bamber Bridge via Lostock Hall (past the loco shed etc.) and enter Preston by the "Bird Cage"; this was the nickname used by railway staff for the large girder bridge over the river Ribble. The usual route coming this way into Preston was around the back through No. 1 Platform and out on the Down Through road past Pitt Street sidings. These former carriage sidings near the high blue brick wall would in later years be the diesel stabling point, and it was here we would see our first examples of the English Electric Type 4's, such as *Empress of England.* The Down Through line would become the Down Blackpool Slow line as we went past the engine sheds, giving us the best possible view right into the sheds. Travelling via the Down Slow line from Fishergate Bridge, that is to say from Preston No. 4 signal box, would give us the same effect as the Down Slow slipped into the Down Blackpool Slow again by the side of the shed. The smaller shed area by the main line always seemed to be a bit of a storage point for engines even before the fire in June 1960. Slipping quietly round the corner of the shed on the Blackpool slow line we would always make the best use of the couple of minutes or so it took to pass the shed. Engine numbers would be quickly jotted down as the view through the windows of the shed revealed another varied selection of motive power. Rounding the curve here, two things stick out in my mind; firstly, at the rear of the shed, a wall protected shed staff from the running lines and there was nearly always a small group of men having a break from shed duties, having a quick "fag"; leaning over the wall watching the trains go by. In the hectic summer months the endless procession of excursion trains must have given the Preston shed staff plenty to see at this busy junction for Blackpool. The second thing which always comes to mind when thinking of the shed area at Preston is the long red enamel sign to be seen on the left hand side just beyond the shed. The sign in BR maroon proclaimed **"TO BLACKPOOL"** and a long arrow situated beneath the legend ran the full length of the sign. After the somewhat slow journey from East Lancashire, you now felt, upon seeing this sign, that Blackpool was just down the road, and once beyond Maudland, speed would increase dramatically and we would be fairly whisked along to Kirkham. Beyond the deep cutting with its high blue brick retaining wall we would pass Maudland Viaduct signal box, here sometimes if we were over on the Fast line we'd be crossed to the Slow line, but more often than not the signalman, to save time, would keep you running Fast line all the way to Kirkham. Passing over a viaduct we headed out towards Haslam Park. Beneath the viaduct there was always a high volume of road traffic, much of it appearing to be heading for the docks, and as we gathered speed across the viaduct, looking over to the left we could view the cranes and boats some distance away at Preston Docks!

Farington Curve Junction

(above) Holiday relief 4.7.64 Class 4 passenger tanks often worked excursions and summer relief trains to the seaside. Here, **42153** drops down the slope from Lostock Hall to Farington Curve Junction with a relief from East Lancashire. In the foreground are the lines from Moss Lane Junction (Liverpool). *Peter Fitton.*

(below) Brush 2's on the Sheffield. In a view taken from the opposite side of the line to the one above and slightly nearer to the junction, we see two of Sheffield Darnalls new Brush type 2's slipping beneath Flag Lane bridge with 1X19, a summer Saturday's excursion to Blackpool in **August 1962**. *Geoff Robinson.*

(centre) Farington Curve Junction signalbox. Wedged tightly against Bee Lane bridge, this grimy little signal box was located between the fast and slow lines of the West coast main line not too far south from Preston station. Many is the night we've crept up to the dimly gas lit cabin before bearing right for the climb up to Lostock Hall engine sheds. **(above) Dropping down to the junction 6.7.63.** No **73162,** of Wakefield (a summer season transfer) drifts towards Flag Lane bridge with 1M07 from Castleford, which was heading for Blackpool Central. **(below)** "Crab" **42901,** with a curious leak of steam from the dome, approaches the point where the Liverpool line joins the East Lancs Line at Farington Curve Junction with 1T74, a Whitefield to Blackpool special which had travelled via Bury Bolton Street, Ramsbottom and Accrington South curve. *British Railways and Peter Fitton*

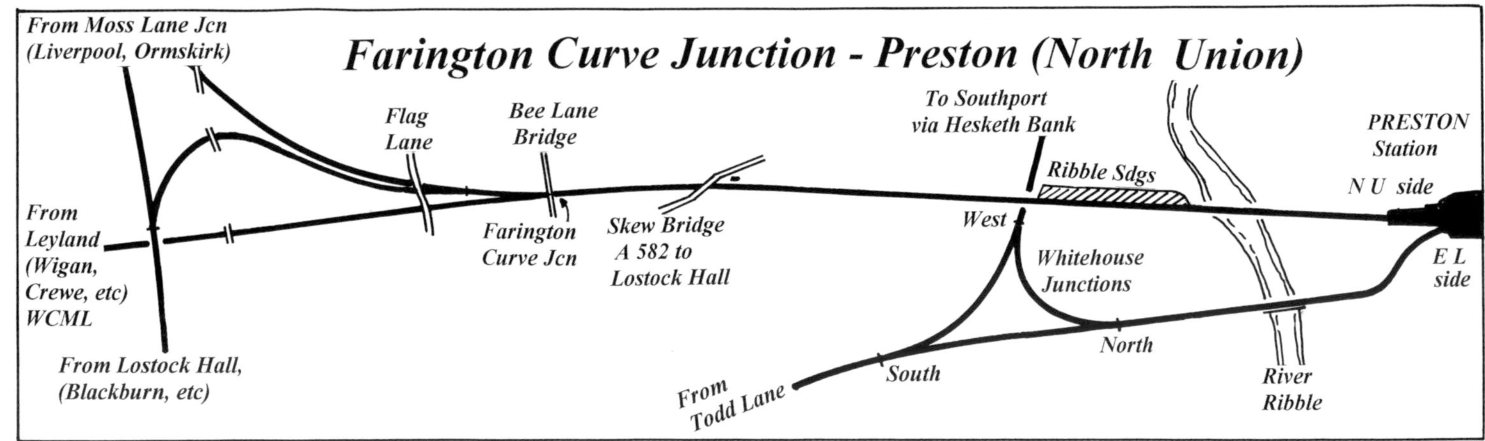

(above) Soled and heeled. A Horwich trials engine, straight framed "Crab" **42952,** brings special C750 over the junction at Farington curve. Bolton men would be working this wakes week excursion using the ex-works locomotive until it was time for it to return home "run-in" to Nuneaton. **(right)** In a view the opposite way looking back towards the junction and Preston, **46140** *The King's Royal Rifle Corps* is seen heading a stopping train to Manchester on 9th May 1964.

Brian Barlow and Arnold Battson.

LE to Lostock Hall. On 24th August 1963, a very tidy looking **70053,** *Moray Firth*, makes for Lostock Hall depot after working 1L23, a Crewe to Windermere service. Note that the semaphore signals are still there in 1963, but by early 1964 had been replaced by colour lights. Farington Curve Junction signalbox itself remained in use until the spring of 1973.
Peter Fitton.

On the Up Fast. Fleetwood's **42867** leaves Preston with a Fleetwood to Manchester express C351. Trains from the fishing port on the Fylde could easily be detected by the inclusion of fish vans next to the engine. In this view, Farington Curve Junction is behind the camera to the left whilst Skew Bridge and the line into Preston are seen behind the train.
Jim Davenport.

(below) Skew Bridge signalbox. We are now at the other side of Skew Bridge, where the goods lines seen in the foreground begin their run along to the Ribble Sidings yard. On the fast line, a Duchess "Pacific" is about to pass a big wheeled Compound 4-4-0 working a Manchester to Blackpool service. *R. B. Holden*

Factory Lane, Preston. A popular spotting point with many enthusiasts, Factory Lane was to be found between Skew Bridge signalbox and Preston's Ribble Sidings marshalling yard. **46228** *Duchess of Rutland* heads south with the combined 9.00a.m. from Perth and the 10.50a.m. from Workington to Euston, a mere 17 coach load. No wonder the main line firemen looked like bean poles, but it was all in a days work forty years ago, when this view was taken on **4th May 1957**. *Tom Lewis.*

Entering PRESTON *via the North Union side*

46251 ***City of Nottingham.*** The engine that graced the cover of the November 1962 Ian Allan A.B.C. book for the L M Region, slips effortlessly into Preston with 1S77, the 3.40p.m. (Fridays Only) Crewe to Glasgow service, on 24th July 1964. The engine became a bit of a railtour favourite during the last years that the class operated, hence the clean state we see here. Across on **page 15 (bottom right),** we see the same train now running down platform four at Preston. These big "Staniers" were withdrawn to keep the accountants happy. They were steam tight, not a blow anywhere, and rode like a Rolls Royce. Their diesel replacements were less efficient, noisy and rough at speed and used excessive fuel, and therefore proved costly to maintain.

Arnold Battson.

PRESTON

(above) Bank Hall Caprotti. Don Greenwood took some superb views around Preston. From his office window in Pitt Street he had a grand stand view of the North end of the station. Many happy hours would also be spent on the platforms of the station and it was here at the south end of platform 5 that he snapped **44743** on **Friday 24th June 1960** as it worked a morning express from Liverpool Exchange to Blackpool. On the left towards the rear of the train is Preston's no. 1 signal box, whilst over to the right is Christian Road goods depot. *D.T.Greenwood (courtesy Rail Archive Stephenson)*

The avoiding lines! Whilst our attention was aimed primarily at the passenger traffic, it was hard to ignore the activity over on the west side of the station where the Up and Down Through lines catered for a variety of trains not requiring the sanctuary of the platforms. In the view above, looking north from between the Up Through and Down Slow lines, the pair of through lines is framed oy the signal gantry as they curve their way past the elevated position of No 2A signal box, which also enjoyed a bird's eye view of the coming and goings on the steeply graded single line Ribble Branch branch which served Preston Docks. The island that served the Up and Down Slow lines (Platforms 1&2) appears behind the right hand upright of the gantry, a comparitvely rare view of the time it served passenger trains before services were concentrated on platforms to the east. For once, all seems quiet, although watchful eyes peer from the gloom of platform four. Christian Road Goods Depot is to the left of the picture. *BR(LMR)*

Preston, the main Southbound platform (no. 6). On the right we have two views of the main southbound platform. At the top is **45526** *Morecambe and Heysham* waiting departure in the late 1950's and below is one of Blackpool's Compounds **41189** on a "stopper" to Manchester in the summer of 1955.

Pictures by J Yates (R. B Holden) and Arnold Battson

PRESTON

from the air

Up amongst the clouds. A typically sunny summer's day at Preston helps us to portray the way things looked from the air. Right at the base of the picture is the former West Lancashire Railway's Fishergate terminus. This was used latterly as a storage point for Silcocks animal feeds. Following the main road up the picture (Fishergate) note how the Strand Road branch weaves its way down from the station area to the docks, passing at an angle beneath Fishergate. The station itself is seen in the centre of the picture. Rows of 12 ton vans fill Christian Road goods depot and the very modern and up to date looking buildings of the Post Office sorting offices stand out against the surrounding structures. On the right side of the picture we see the main lines coming in from the South and the East Lancs Lines curving in to meet them in the station. The Park Hotel with access via Vicars bridge separates these lines. The East Lancs Line was of course from Todd Lane and Bamber Bridge etc., The extensive goods yard behind the station was the former EL yard at Butler Street, which is now sadly just a car park and supermarket. To the left of the bridge at Fishergate we can see the coal yards at Corporation Street and Dock Street.

Aerofilms Ltd.

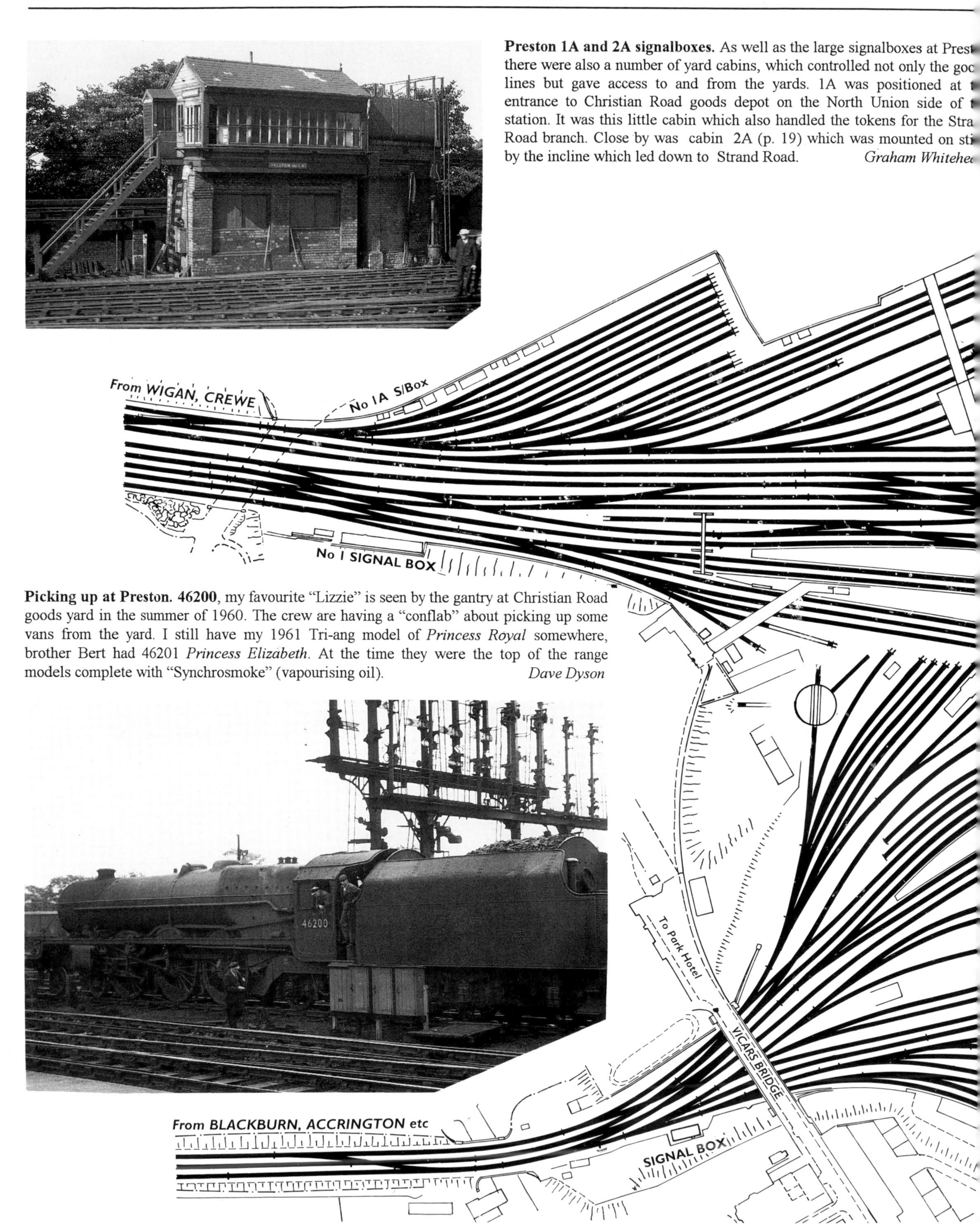

Preston 1A and 2A signalboxes. As well as the large signalboxes at Prest there were also a number of yard cabins, which controlled not only the goo lines but gave access to and from the yards. 1A was positioned at t entrance to Christian Road goods depot on the North Union side of t station. It was this little cabin which also handled the tokens for the Stra Road branch. Close by was cabin 2A (p. 19) which was mounted on sti by the incline which led down to Strand Road. *Graham Whitehe*

Picking up at Preston. 46200, my favourite "Lizzie" is seen by the gantry at Christian Road goods yard in the summer of 1960. The crew are having a "conflab" about picking up some vans from the yard. I still have my 1961 Tri-ang model of *Princess Royal* somewhere, brother Bert had 46201 *Princess Elizabeth*. At the time they were the top of the range models complete with "Synchrosmoke" (vapourising oil). *Dave Dyson*

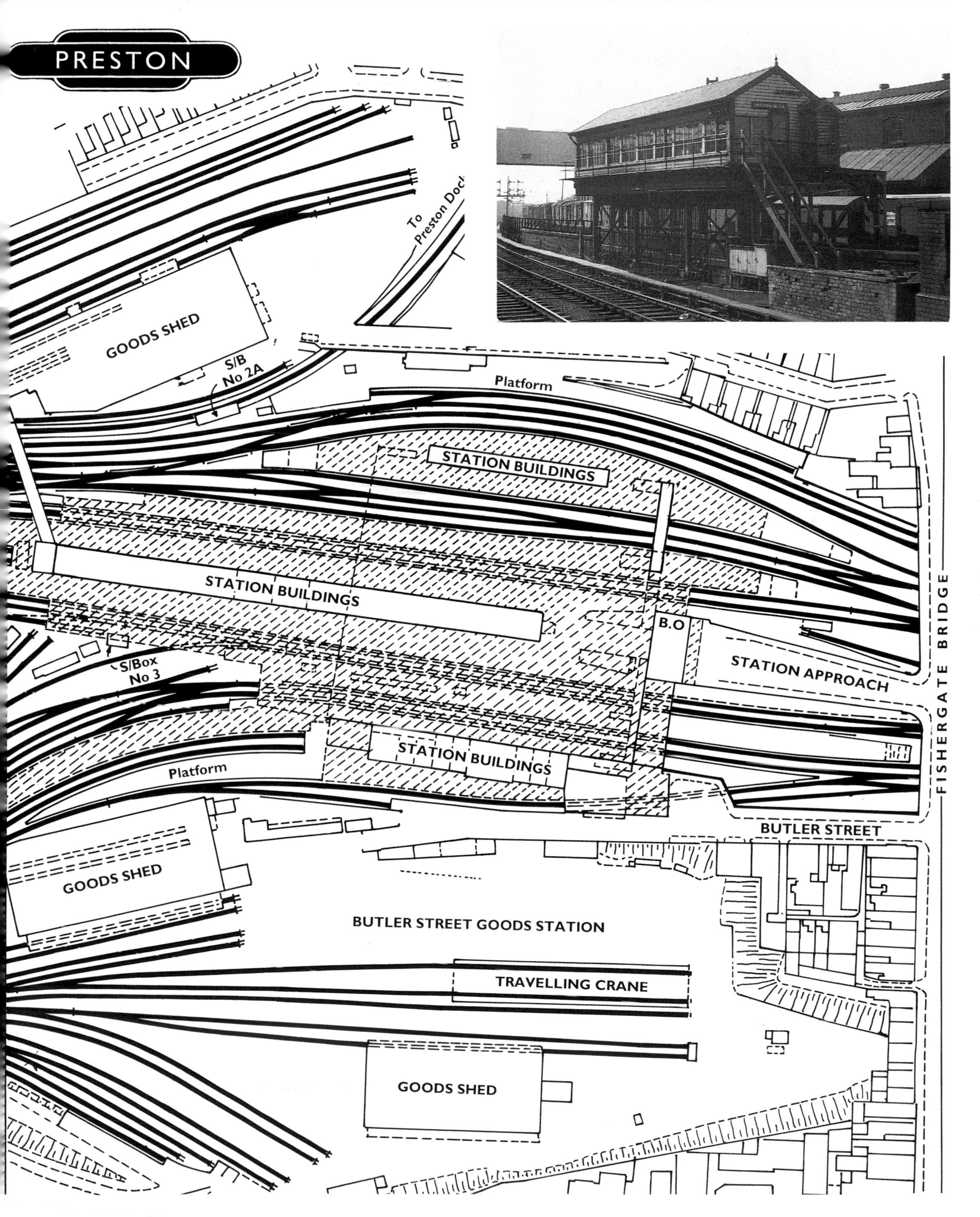
PRESTON
To
Preston Doc
GOODS SHED
S/B
No 2A
Platform
STATION BUILDINGS
STATION BUILDINGS
B.O
STATION APPROACH
FISHERGATE BRIDGE
S/Box
No 3
STATION BUILDINGS
Platform
BUTLER STREET
GOODS SHED
BUTLER STREET GOODS STATION
TRAVELLING CRANE
GOODS SHED

Preston
E L
(East Lancs)

Vicars Bridge. Two views here looking both ways off Vicars Bridge. **(left)** **42844** of Fleetwood hauls a freight round the tight curve into the "E L" side of Preston station. **(Below)** looking towards Butler Street warehouses and the E L side platforms, we can see Bank Hall's famous Patriot **45517**, an engine that always seemed well cared for, coming out with a Liverpool bound train. **90584,** with a tender full of "nutty slack" is doing a shunt on a trip freight.

Arnold Battson (2).

(above) E L Carriage sidings. A couple of Class 4 passenger tanks sit in the carriage sidings on the East Lancs Curve. The main train shed dominates the scene behind; note the tightly curved East Lancs Main lines, (just above the right hand engine's boiler). The large solid coach wheels of our excursion train would grind and give off a dull ringing noise as we edged our way round into the station. Once beneath the overall roof of the station, it would become noticeably darker, our engine often sending glowing cinders up to the roof as it barked its way towards Fishergate Bridge. Looking left as we entered the train shed we would have seen a similar view to the one reproduced here of Britannia **70046** *Anzac*, on the Barrow - Euston. *Tom Lewis and Peter Fitton.*

Preston no. 7 platform, 4.5.64. A grimy *Duchess of Rutland* **46228** awaits departure with the 7.00a.m. Carlisle to Crewe. By 1964 these big Stanier Pacifics were "tab-ending" on a variety of short haul jobs in the Crewe, Liverpool and Carlisle areas. It was a sad end for such thoroughbred machines; they looked so much like caged lions. *Arnold Battson.*

Queuing up at Preston. Preston's no. 4 platform plays host to *Clan Frazer* 72003 as well as a preceding excursion service. The "Clan" (note how close he is to the rear of the other train) was working a Liverpool to Glasgow service in the summer of 1961. Those early "Clans", 72000 - 4 , of Polmadie, were regular visitors to Preston, Liverpool, Manchester and the Fylde coast. Sadly they became victims of the cutbacks made at the end of the summer timetable in 1962 and all were stored pending overhauls they would never receive. Despite pleas from the shedmaster at Carlisle Kingmoor to allow them to join the others already there (72005 - 9), those early members of the class were cut up during 1963 at Darlington Works. The little inset picture shows the curious inspectors building that sat on the main line platforms at Preston, note the curved doors. *Arnold Battson. Inset by Graham Whitehead.*

"Tanks" for the memory

Working the locals. Before we give the impression that Preston was full of "Duchesses", "Lizzies" and "Clans", etc., and little else, let us show just a couple of the great many tank engines which formed the everyday scene prior to the advent of the diesel railcars. **(left) 84016** (note the very thin tyres) of Fleetwood, awaits departure from Platform 3). The mighty Fowler 2-6-4 tanks were known to engine men as "Crab" tanks, and **(below), 42402** of Barrow in Furness shed simmers in one of the middle roads between trips. The later ones with side window cabs were quite rare. *Dave Dyson.*

By Fishergate bridge. To see a "Lizzie" was one thing; to see an ex-works one was, in the words of singer Eddy Cochran, "Something Else". Here, **46206** *Princess Marie Louise,* gives the briefest of wheel slips as she sets off on the trip north from Preston's no. 5 platform. The old driver is clearly enjoying his work. Probably the train is a heavy summer relief, hence the sanders, but soon he'll be "winding the old girl up" as he leaves the Preston suburbs behind and heads for the Lakeland hills. **(below)** Looking forward from platform 5, we see the bridge at Fishergate. The buildings to the top left are the ornate offices of County Hall, and looking to the right beneath the bridge, is Preston's no. 4 signalbox. A Jubilee (5X) is about to enter the station and can be seen passing by Pitt Street carriage sidings. *Dave Dyson and British Railways.*

PRESTON

FISHERGATE BRIDGE

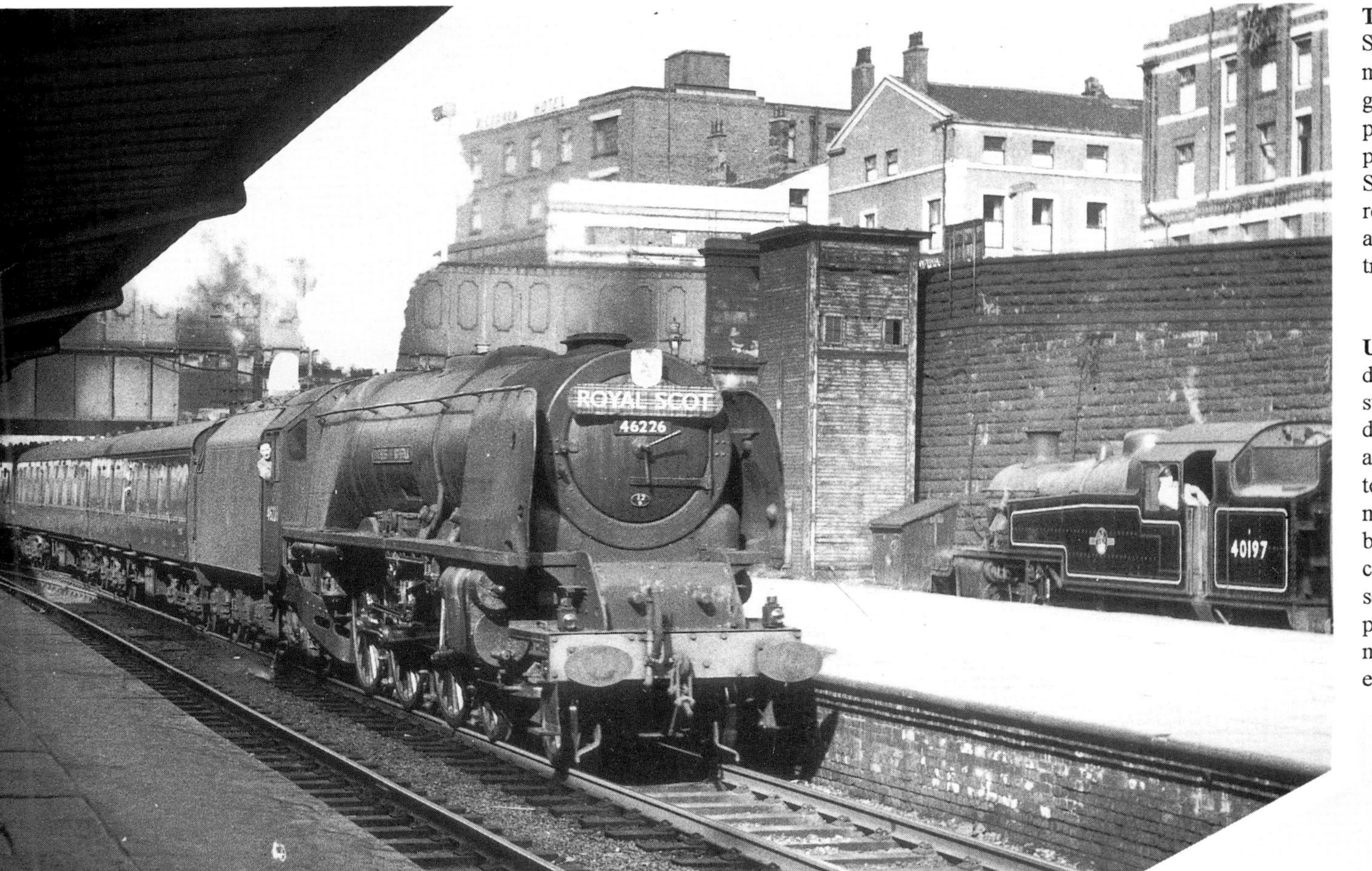

The Up "Royal Scot", April 1959. Sounding like a well oiled sewing machine, **46226** *Duchess of Norfolk* glides briskly through Preston's no. 7 platform with the "Up Scot". Over on platform eight the driver of the little Stanier class 3 tank **40197** seems more interested in the shunt move he is about to make with the stock off his train from Southport.

Arnold Battson.

Up on the bridge (1). Fishergate bridge is a huge construction of stone and steel, which today looks the same as it did during our trips well over 35 years ago. In this view we are looking down towards Fishergate Hill. The station main entrance is over to the left, just by the Austin pick-up. The ornate council offices are over to the right as seen earlier. It was from this elevated position that Don Greenwood took so many fine pictures during the 1950s etc. (see page 28). *British Railways.*

PRESTON

Fishergate bridge

City of London **on the Lakes Express**. Geoff Robinson's photographic efforts at Great Harwood ensured that we were able to portray fully the journey round the Padiham - Great Harwood loop in part one of this series. This particular view at Preston of **46245** is Geoff's favourite picture, of which there is sadly now no negative. Even sadder is the fact that such a fine engine as "6245" was allowed to go to the melting pot. *Geoff Robinson.*

BRITISH RAILWAYS

Up on the bridge (2). The opposite view up on Fishergate bridge to the one on page 26 is this scene taken from the corner of Pitt Street. Look at the sheer size and scale of the stone columns and the steelwork as compared to the passers-by and note how clean the area is in this 1963 view. *British Railways.*

Beyond the bridge. Leaving the station behind, we would head out to Maudlands Junction. The immediate area beyond the station seemed full of buildings which towered above us. This particular view was taken from Don Greenwood's office window in the Council Offices in Pitt Street which faced the railway at this point. Over on the other side of the lines we see the Victoria Hotel (top left). On the retaining wall lower down to the left note the large red enamel sign announcing "Preston 100 yards". The two engines seen here are Edge Hill's **45508** and Rose Grove's **45209.** They were about to work a combined Liverpool and Manchester to Glasgow and Edinburgh express in June 1957. *Don Greenwood courtesy of Rail Archive Stephenson.*

A last look back. We would always "man" the windows leaving Preston, shouting out the numbers of passing engines to Dad, who, with notepad on knee, would quickly record them, usually in pencil. Sometimes they would come fast and furious as we neared the engine sheds by Fylde Junction. 47472, 42296, 45313, 44894, 75049, 42867, 47413, 46243, 46136, 45627, and so it would go on. Quite often we'd be sorting numbers out and cross checking notes all the way to Lea Road. **45627** *Sierra Leone* leaves Preston with excursion 1T82, from Liverpool to Blackpool.

Ray Farrell.

Approaching Maudlands Junction. Here we have the second view by Fleetwood engineman Tony Bretherton. Taken from the cab of a little 84XXX class tank on a journey back to Fleetwood. Maudlands Junction can be seen just ahead by the two bracket signals, which were adjacent to the no. 5 signalbox. St. Walburge's Church spire dominates the scene as always and to the left we see the engine sheds, which had become a storage point by the time Tony took this summer 1964 view. About this time, **46257** *City of Salford* would soon become a short term resident in the shed whilst awaiting that final call. *Tony Bretherton.*

Fishergate bridge to Fylde Junction

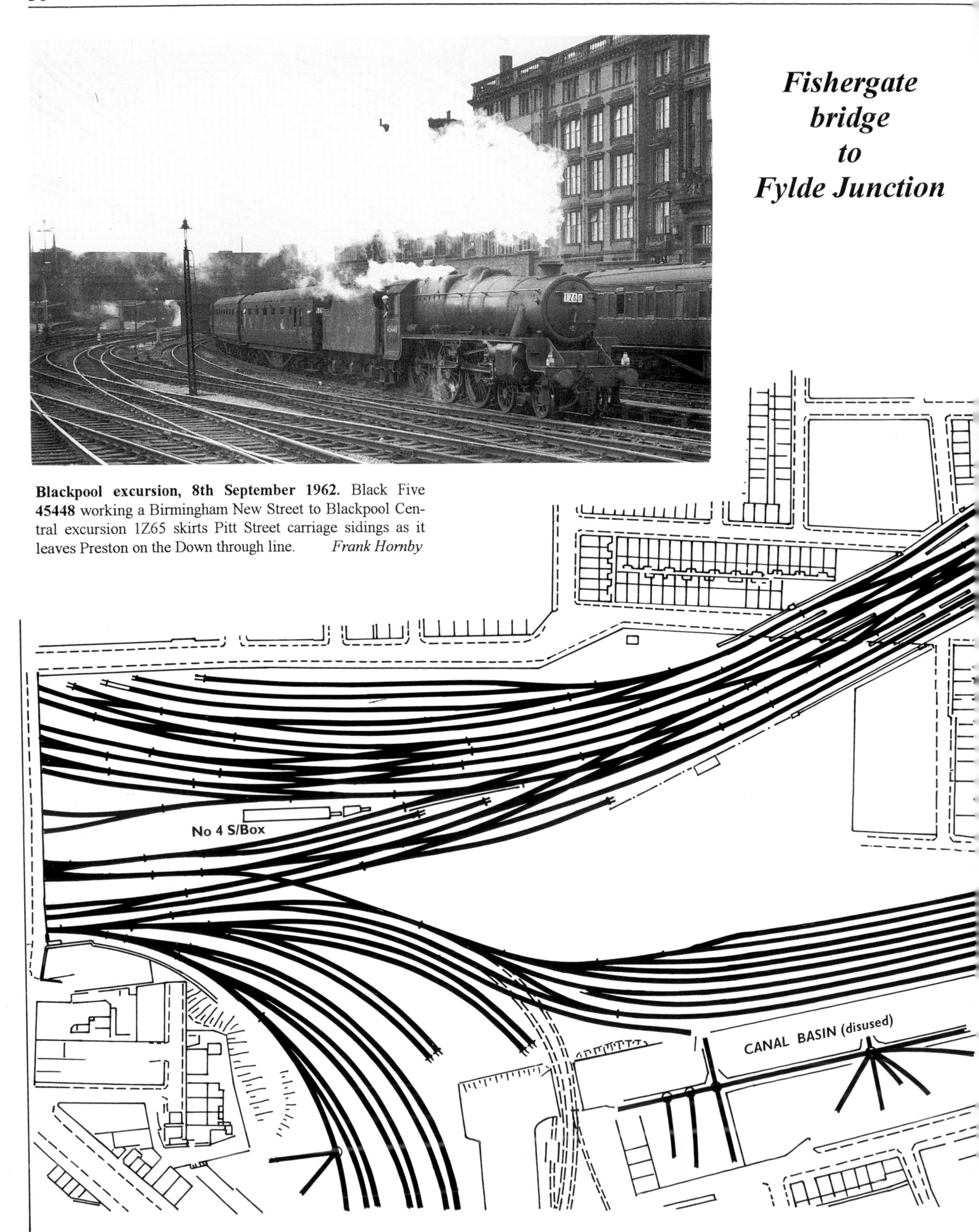

Blackpool excursion, 8th September 1962. Black Five **45448** working a Birmingham New Street to Blackpool Central excursion 1Z65 skirts Pitt Street carriage sidings as it leaves Preston on the Down through line. *Frank Hornby*

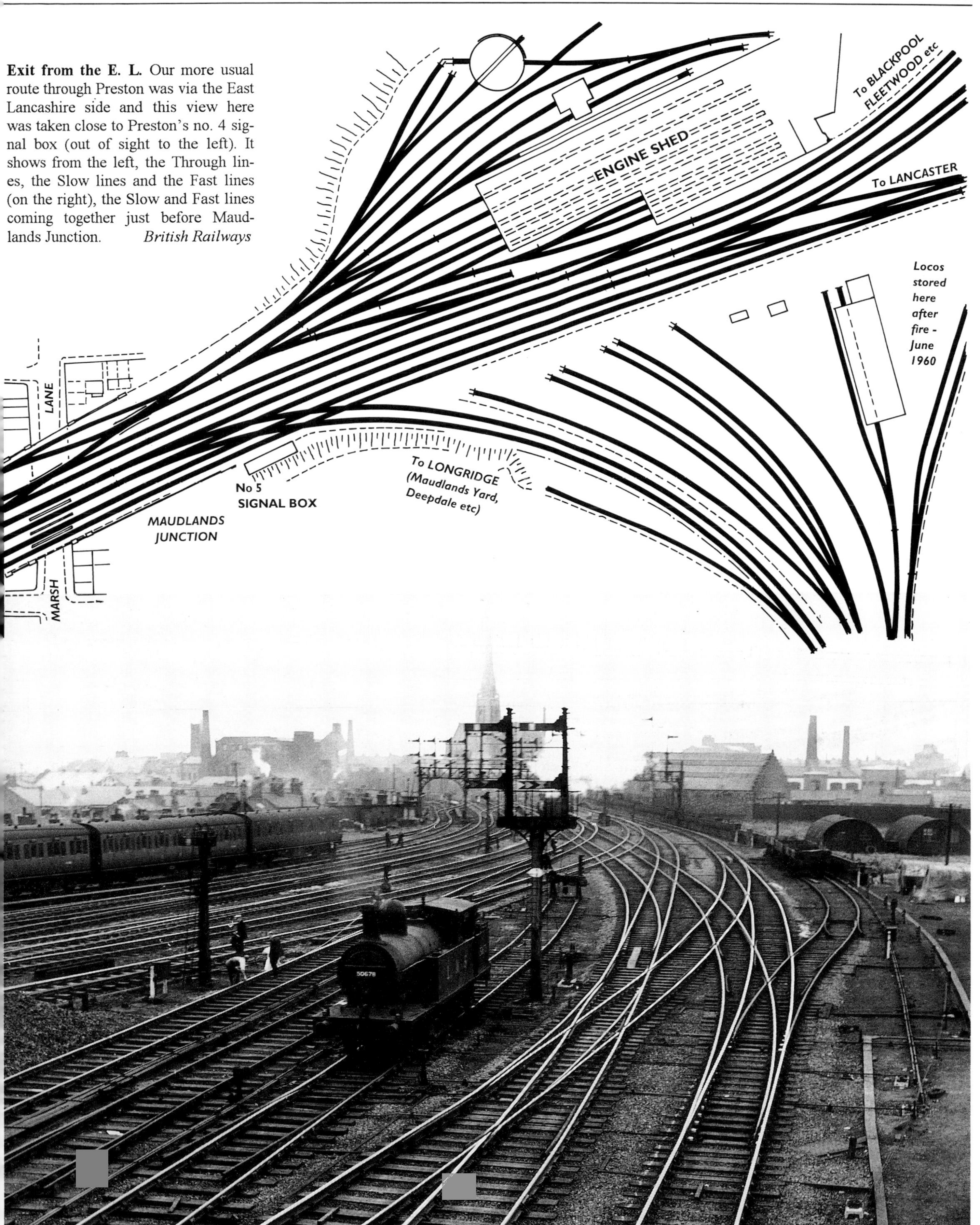

Exit from the E. L. Our more usual route through Preston was via the East Lancashire side and this view here was taken close to Preston's no. 4 signal box (out of sight to the left). It shows from the left, the Through lines, the Slow lines and the Fast lines (on the right), the Slow and Fast lines coming together just before Maudlands Junction. *British Railways*

PRESTON'S M.P.D

and Maudlands Junction

Maudlands 8.9.56. On a lovely September morning in 1956, the railway at Maudlands seems deserted, a most unusual sight, but it helps us to show the very extensive track layout at this point. The lines again read Down and Up Through, Down and Up Slow and Down and Up Fast, with the branch to Deepdale and Longridge bearing away to the right (off the Slow lines) by the large no. 5 signalbox. The warehouse in Maudlands yard can be seen over to the right of the signalbox and it was behind this large structure that the engines damaged in the Preston shed fire of the 28th June 1960 were stored pending repair in July of that year, (see page 34). In this summer 1956 view, the shed appears quite busy and as a rule, as we drew near to the shed on our way to the Fylde Coast, it was always very easy to note the numbers of the engines on the shed roads and even the odd one tucked in the shed would be visible through the broken windows alongside the main lines. The inset picture **(bottom left - opposite)** shows the state of the shed immediately after the fire in June 1960. **78037** and **42707** are still in the position they occupied when the fire swept through the shed. The heat was apparently so intense that in certain places the metal work twisted and distorted out of shape. *British Railways and Don Greenwood (courtesy of Rail Archive Stephenson).*

(Below right) BR Class 4 **75049**, formerly of Accrington shed, was a Bank Hall engine by the time Peter Fitton took this view of her working the 9a.m. Blackpool Central to Liverpool Exchange penultimate service on the 4th September 1964. *Peter Fitton.*

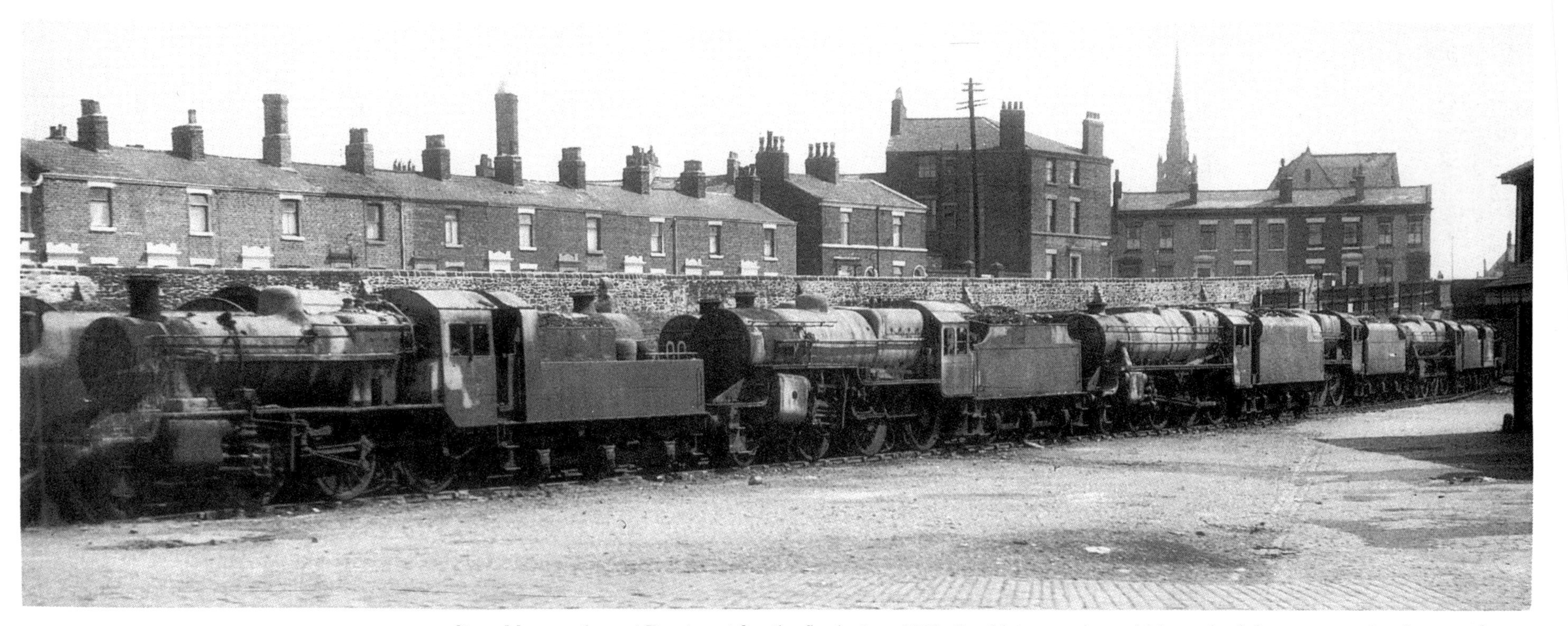

Stored at Maudlands

Stored locomotives at Preston. After the fire in June 1960, the thirteen engines which received damage were stored across from the shed in Maudlands goods yard. **(above)** It was here that we saw them on our holiday travels during July of that year. The locomotives were 78037, behind which is 45675 and 73128. The nearest line then continues with 42707 - 45065, behind which are 46161 - 45315 - 48414 - 49104. In the next few years the shed itself became a storage point. **(below left)** Lancaster Green Ayre Crab **42776** is seen in the shed together with **42931** and **42938** in the early summer of 1964. **(Below right) 49008** and **49447** stand outside the shed on Sunday, 16th September 1962.

Don Greenwood, Bert Holland and Peter Fitton.

seat), Chris Spring (on running plate), together with Paul Claxton and Richard Davis take a last look round the stored Patriots in Preston Shed, before they were despatched to Crewe and Horwich works for scrapping in 1963. **(Below right) 45551** was seen on 16th September 1962 and **(below left) 46257** on 23rd September 1964.

45530* Sir Frank Ree
45531* Sir Frederick Harrison
45532* Illustrious
45533 Lord Rathmore
45534* E. Tootal Broadhurst
45535* Sir Herbert Walker, K.C.B.
45536* Private W. Wood, V.C.
45538 Giggleswick
45540* Sir Robert Turnbull
45543 Home Guard
45545* Planet
45547
45550

TOTAL: 26

6P5F & 7P "Jubilee" 4-6-0

6P5F, introduced 1934. Stanier L.M.S. taper boiler development of the "Patriot" class.
† Fitted with double chimney.
* 7P, introduced 1942. Rebuilt with larger boiler and double chimney.

Weight Locomotive: 79 tons 11 cwt, 82 tons 0 cwt*
Boiler pressure 225 lb sq in, 250 lb sq in*
Cylinders Three, 17" × 26"
Driving wheel diameter 6' 9"
Tractive effort 26,610 lb, 29,570 lb*
Valve gear Walschaerts (piston valves)

45552 Silver Jubilee
45553 Canada
45554 Ontario
45555 Quebec
45556 Nova Scotia
45557 New Brunswick
45558 Manitoba
45559 British Columbia
45560 Prince Edward Island
45561 Saskatchewan
45562 Alberta
45563 Australia
45564 New South Wales
45565 Victoria
45566 Queensland
45567 South Australia
45568 Western Australia
45569 Tasmania
45570 New Zealand
45571 South Africa
45572 Eire
45573 Newfoundland
45574 India
45575 Madras
45576 Bombay
45577 Bengal
45578 United Provinces
45579 Punjab
45580 Burma
45581 Bihar and Orissa
45582 Central Provinces
45583 Assam
45584 North West Frontier
45585 Hyderabad
45586 Mysore
45587 Baroda
45588 Kashmir
45589 Gwalior
45590 Travancore
45591 Udaipur
45592 Indore
45593 Kholapur
45594 Bhopal
45595 Southern Rhodesia
45596† Bahamas
45597 Barbados

Class 7P 4-6-0 No. 45535 Sir Herbert Walker, K.C.B. [R. W. Martin

Class 6P5F 4-6-0 No. 45596 Bahamas (with double chimney) [D. C. Smith

Class 6P5F 4-6-0 No. 45698 Mars [G. W. Morrison

30

In Store. Between 1961 and 1964 the disused Loco. shed at Preston played host to a number of locomotives. Virtually all were redundant and ready for their last trip to the breakers yard. Around a dozen Patriots, almost a similar number of "Super D's", together with Lancaster Green Ayre's old Crab's could all be seen in the shed at varying times. Later in 1964, 46257 *City of Salford*, 45579 *Punjab* and "Scot" 46168 were there for a short while.

Don Greenwood (R.A.S.), Arnold Battson and Peter Fitton.

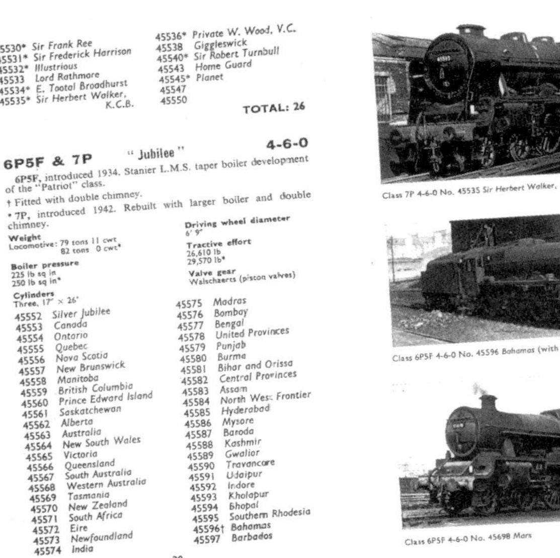

On the water troughs at Lea Road

Taking water at Lea Road. The water troughs between Lea Road and Salwick were in fact situated on both sides of Lea Lane Bridge (see map below on page 41). Effectively the water troughs began close to Constable Lane signalbox and ended near to Salwick no.1 signal cabin, this latter block post being the one which gave access to the sidings at the UKAEA plant at Springfields. The term in the caption heading again comes from my old workmate Ken Bradshaw, who was a "Passed man" at Fleetwood for many years. When we used to talk about the "road" to Blackpool the water troughs were always referred to as being at Lea Road and over the years I've always tended to follow Ken's line of thinking, therefore as far as I'm concerned it will always be "Lea Road troughs". I don't think it would be possible to find a better picture that fully portrays the scene on the water troughs as it was during our excursion years, than the one kindly loaned by Brian Stephenson which is from the superb Stan Garth collection. The picture taken in August 1954 is truly full of the atmosphere of the period. The warm but overcast summer's day, the mixed smells of warm oil, sulpherous coal, and newly mown hay from the surrounding fields that would come wafting in through the open carriage window. As always, Dad would "yank" up the compartment window using the thick leather strap as we approached the water troughs, and as a rule, shortly afterwards, the water would come flooding back from the tender tank giving us a brief impression of a cloud burst. Being next to the engine we were first in line for a drenching when the tank overflowed and the poor old fireman couldn't lift the scoop. Here, the old driver's eased off to take a leisurely dip with this Manchester - Blackpool excursion C860. He's clearly being considerate to both his mate and the passengers. One final point, if you look carefully to the right side of the picture, just behind the coaches it is possible to see the isolated signal cabin at Constable Lane, which could only be reached by walking across

Deflecting Dome
Operating Handle
Shaft & Counterweight
Deflector Linkage
Trough
Riser Pipe
Scoop (lowered)
Deflector

HOW AN ENGINE TAKES WATER AT SPEED

Topping the tank up. If the tender tank was still reasonably full, then dipping the scoop at Lea Road in order to save time taking water on shed at Blackpool would undoubtedly lead to the tank overflowing, as would hitting the troughs too fast. It may have ensured a good pick-up but once down the scoop would be a devil to wind up again against the sheer pressure of water. Quite often the driver would leave his post to help his young mate who would be straining on the winding handle of the water scoop. All too often the scene on the footplate could resemble the deck of a trawler in high seas. I can well imagine that on quite a few occasions trains will have been seen passing Kirkham with the crew stripped down to their string vests and underpants as their overhauls dried off on the boiler back plate. Here Black Five **45246** gives us a good impression of "Niagara Falls" as it passes over the troughs with the 4.55p.m. from Manchester Victoria to Blackpool North on Monday 31st August 1964. The bridge in the background carries Lea Lane and marked the halfway spot along the water troughs. **(right)** Blackpool Rigby Road driver Harold Blundy is seen smiling cheerfully for the camera as he heads for Kirkham. At the time this view was taken by his mate Don Rutter, Harold was on local work (light duties) following a bash on the neck from a "shackle" (coupling) whilst attempting to " tie" his engine onto a train.

Peter Fitton and Don Rutter

SEASIDE, EVENING AND OTHER EXCURSIONS To
BLACKPOOL

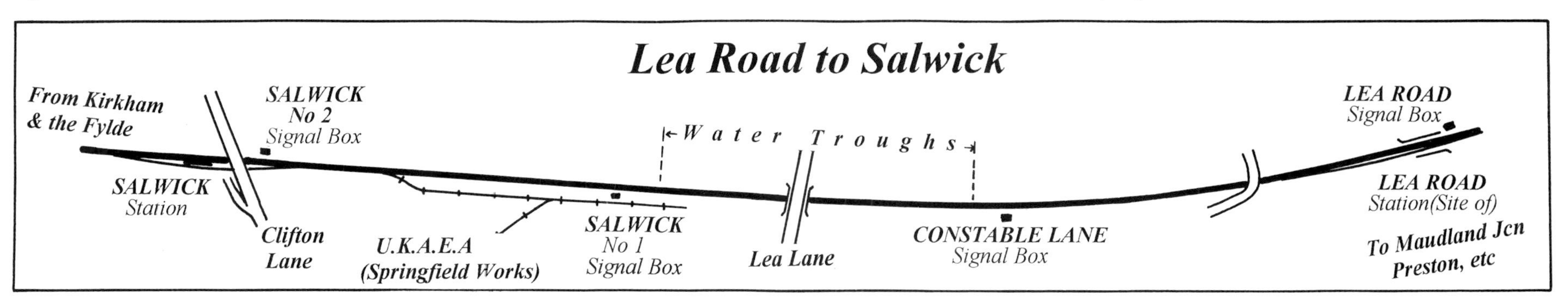

Salwick station. The driver of BR 4 **76087** is certainly "chopping 'em off" as he rattles through Salwick on the Down Fast line heading for Kirkham and the Fylde with the 10.55am Manchester Victoria to Blackpool North on the 8th August 1964. This diagram working also saw the engine cover a trip round to Fleetwood before it headed back to Manchester. **(left)** Blackpool "Passed" man Don Rutter, with the regulator "Up in the roof", is portrayed dashing along towards Kirkham. Don, together with a great many other footplatemen remembers vividly the days when trains would race on the four track section from Preston through Salwick to Kirkham South Junction.*PeterFitton/Don Rutter*

Salwick, a last look. Looking every bit like one of our excursion outings to the Lancashire Coast, the Black Five seen here **45150**, was in fact working the 12.05p.m. from Manchester Victoria to Blackpool Central (C216) and was about to call at Salwick station on a warm sunny June day in 1959. **(below)** 1T59, an excursion from Manchester also heading for Blackpool Central, slips quickly by Salwick on the Fast lines with **45522** *Prestatyn*, as the motive power. Over on the Slow line Blackpool's **45464** struggles to keep up whilst working 1T05 from Meir (Stoke - on - Trent) on Whit Monday (18th May) 1964. *John E. Porter and Peter Fitton.*

From Salwick to Kirkham, part of the route was tree lined, and this wooded section hemmed in the smoke and such from the occasional lineside fire, causing us to pass through a grey haze as we accelerated towards Spen Lane and Treales on the approach to Kirkham. By the time Spen Lane was passed, we were rolling along a very wide but shallow cutting, the only overbridge being by the nearby Cardwell Farm. The bridge had brick abutments with substantial main girders to span the four tracks. Dowbridge (underbridge) was passed shortly afterwards and two more overbridges, close together, would quickly bring us to Kirkham. The second of these two carried Moorside Lane. This structure consisted of red brick except for the main girders. Grass could always be seen growing merrily from the joints of the crumbling masonry. Treales signal box, just to the right of this bridge, controlled both the Fast and Slow lines at this point. Just after leaving Treales, looking over the fields to the left, the spire of the church at Kirkham could be seen, followed soon afterwards by Kirkham South Junction, which would be approached with a noticeable drop in speed if we were travelling on the Slow line. Swinging through the curves near to Kirkham and Wesham station, we would always see the outlines of two figures, painters holding a ladder that advertised the name of Sissons, one of the major paint firms of the time. The Sissons company name was displayed at Kirkham and the sign was in the field that lay between the church spire and the railway embankment. Upon first sighting the church spire and the painters, dad would give an authoritative nod and proudly point out in a deep tone, "Kirkham". Seeing the two flat capped painters and the spire was again something that we looked forward to seeing year after year. The sleepy looking town of Kirkham was over on the left hand side of the line whilst Wesham was to the right, a familiar landmark of course being the Hospital tower with the pointed roof, now long gone.

1T64 from Blackburn. Also on Whit Monday the 18th May 1964, a set of Rose Grove men took empty stock from Colne via Padiham and Great Harwood to Blackburn to work 1T64 to Blackpool Central, using borrowed 5X **45710** *Irresistable* of Newton Heath shed. As the special headed for the Coast, rail conditions became a touch damp following a brief shower, hence the display of fireworks and the use of the sanders. We don't know who the driver is but he's certainly giving the old girl "some clog" as he passes Whinny Turn Woods west of Salwick. Maybe its Arthur Kennerly in the driving seat, he was known to "make 'em grunt a bit"....!

Peter Fitton.

Fleetwood bound. (left) Lower Darwen•Crab **42722** sprints along past Spen Lane with 3T83 an empty stock special for Fleetwood on 18th August 1962 . Note the fish van next to the engine. A lot of the later fish vans (the Insulfish type), had the slightly longer wheel base and these were allowed to run at 60 mph. Spen Lane signalbox can just be seen to the right of the picture underneath the over bridge which led to Cardwell Farm, which was over on the north side of the line, (see map below on page 47).

(Right) Dowbridge-towards Kirkham. **A** favourite location for photographers on the four track section was this area known as Dowbridge, which was midway between Spen Lane signalbox and Treales on the outskirts of Kirkham. No **42863,** a very tidy looking Hughes/Fowler Crab 2-6-0, brings the last summer seasonal service to Barnsley out of Kirkham past Dowbridge on Saturday 18th August 1962. *Peter Fitton*

Dowbridge towards Salwick. Looking back now towards Spen Lane and Salwick, we see Jubilee **45554** *Ontario* drifting effortlessly westward towards Treales and Kirkham on a very sunny Saturday, 18th August 1962, whilst working 1P38 the 7.38a.m. SO Bletchley to Blackpool North. *Peter Fitton.*

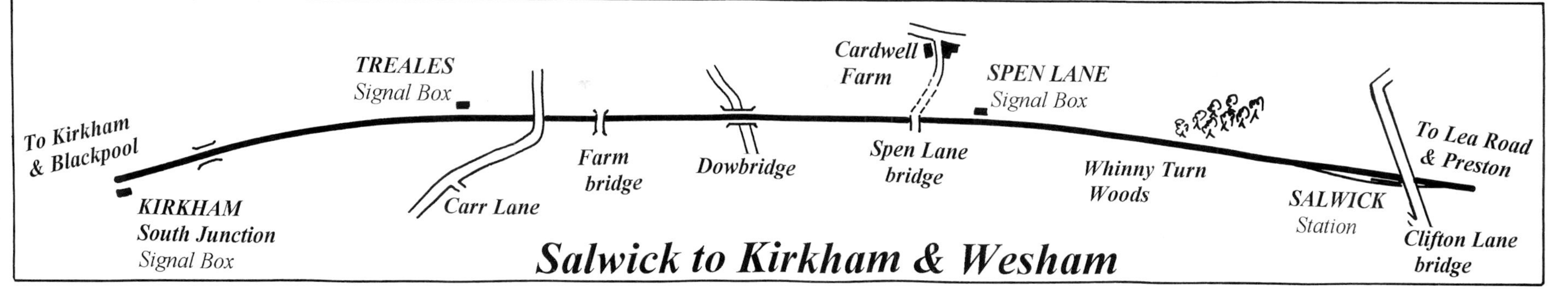

Variety at Dowbridge. (above) W90 the Saturdays only 9.04a.m. Newcastle to Blackpool is unusually viewed from the north side of the line on Saturday 1st August 1959. This service of course travelled over the famous Stainmore route to Tebay, where the locomotive seen here **(43028)** was attached. **(left)** looking towards Kirkham again, we see special C205 with Standard **73014**, the date being the 20th August 1960. In the distance to the left are the two over bridges near Treales signalbox and the water tower at Wesham Park Hospital..

Peter Fitton

1T52 from Colne. Straight framed Crab **42958** on trials from Horwich works has somehow managed to find itself on 1T52 from Colne to Blackpool Central on Whit Monday the 3rd June 1963. I expect it worked the previous night's 9.15p.m. return from Blackpool to Colne, a service with no back working to the Fylde. The engine was therefore usually rostered to work the morning excursion out of Colne to Blackpool Central with Rose Grove depot providing the crew. *Peter Fitton.*

....Salwick to Kirkham

lass 9 on the Leicester. 92107 is ·en between the two over bridges at reales with the 9.50a.m. Leicester to lackpool North working on 20th ugust 1960, which was about the me when "Number Nines" could be ·en on a wide range of passenger ·rvices around the country until som-one pointed out the heavy repair bills ɔr motion and valve and piston parts ıat were becoming evident following rolonged summer use on seasonal ains. **(below)** Just a month after 2107 was photographed approaching reales, **70046** *Anzac* was recorded ɔming out of Kirkham with a relief ɔr Glasgow (1X96). Wesham Park Iospital is clearly visible above reales signalbox in this latter view.

Peter Fitton and Jim Davenport.

The parting of the ways would come as we dipped into a long high sided cutting near to Plumpton Lane bridge, the North line heading off into a similar cutting through Westby woods where Weeton signal box was to be found perched high on the hill next to Plumpton Lane. Incidentally, Weeton army camp was situated nearby to this point and it was here that the old "Green Goddess" Bedford fire engines were stored. These were at one time operated by the Auxiliary Fire Service. The steep high sided cutting at Plumpton needed a high arched bridge to carry the lane over the Marton line, and just beyond this spectacularly high structure, a pipeline, mounted on latticed metal stanchions, crossed the steep embankment. The deep cutting continued on to the next occupation bridge which led up from Moss House Lane to farmland high on the hillside. Once through this bridge, the view opened out on all sides and we could see right across to the coast, and sure enough, over to the right beyond the gasometers of Marton Gasworks was the "Old Vinegar Bottle" (Blackpool Tower), standing dominant on the skyline. Riding now upon an embankment towards Peel, rolling meadows lined both sides of the railway and as excess steam from the boiler and the engine's white exhaust drifted lazily across the open fields, the smell of steam and newly mown hay would be wafting in through the open compartment window In the fields, the little grey Ferguson tractors as well as the Fordson Majors and David Brown Cropmasters could all be seen busily making hay while the sun shone. Approaching Peel, Moss House Farm could be seen resting in the rolling meadow land over on our left hand side. The embankment at Peel swiftly gave way to the overbridge carrying the main A583 into Blackpool. This was followed by another high sided cutting which continued all the way to Marton Gasworks. The gasworks sidings on the right would usually hold a number of ageing wooden high sided coal wagons and the little Peckett shunting engine, almost dwarfed, would be doing its best to shuffle the wagons round the yard.

Plumpton cutting 27th July 1963. Running through the cutting at Plumpton with its huge banked sides was something you never quite forgot, nor was the high arch bridge which carried Plumpton Lane over towards Weeton. This lane continued on past Weeton signal box and over the North line, eventually passing the old Weeton Camp where the "Green Goddess" fire engines are stored. Plumpton cutting, some three quarters of a mile long, was a blaze of colour in the summer months. The sides of the cutting were lush and green and covered in wild flowers. B1 **61161** of "Donny" (Doncaster) is on the "Lincoln" whilst the Black Five coming out of Blackpool is **45371** with an ECS working for Carlisle, and the time of day….it was eight minutes past two in the afternoon.

Peter Fitton

Bridge 102 - Our first view of Blackpool Tower

Bridge 102 - 2nd June 1963. Once beyond the high arch bridge at Plumpton, the deep cutting gave way to open countryside beyond bridge 102. I can still vividly recall the rushing sound as we literally burst out through the bridge "hole" into open countryside. There, over on our right hand side was "The old vinegar bottle", Blackpool Tower, some four and a half miles away at this point, but as clear as a bell on sunny days. In our view **(left)** the tower is just visible above the tender of **45622** *Nyasaland,* as it coasts towards bridge 102 with 1T06 from Nottingham. (the same train is also seen above).

Peter Fitton (2)

Summertime on the Marton Line

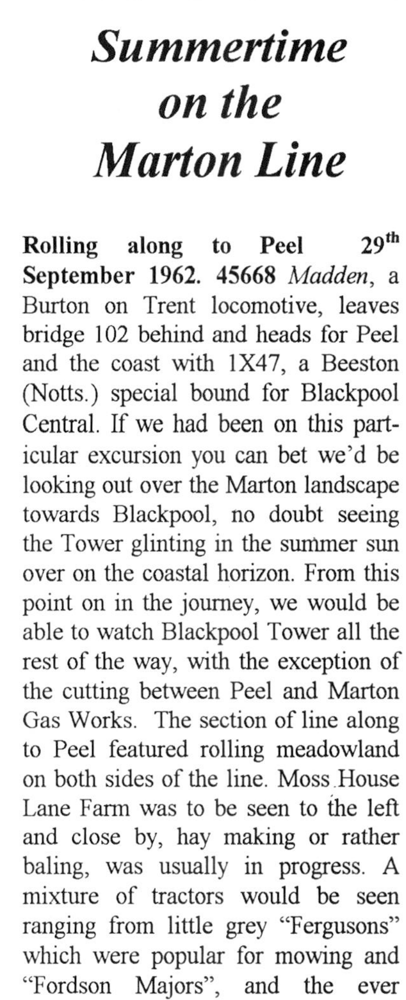

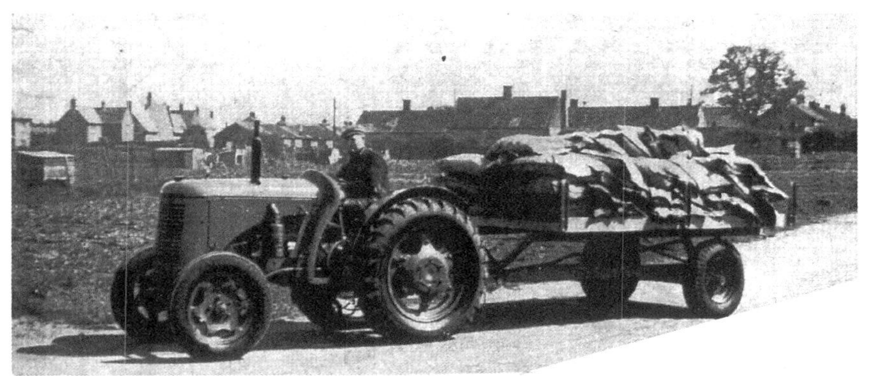

Rolling along to Peel 29th September 1962. 45668 *Madden*, a Burton on Trent locomotive, leaves bridge 102 behind and heads for Peel and the coast with 1X47, a Beeston (Notts.) special bound for Blackpool Central. If we had been on this particular excursion you can bet we'd be looking out over the Marton landscape towards Blackpool, no doubt seeing the Tower glinting in the summer sun over on the coastal horizon. From this point on in the journey, we would be able to watch Blackpool Tower all the rest of the way, with the exception of the cutting between Peel and Marton Gas Works. The section of line along to Peel featured rolling meadowland on both sides of the line. Moss House Lane Farm was to be seen to the left and close by, hay making or rather baling, was usually in progress. A mixture of tractors would be seen ranging from little grey "Fergusons" which were popular for mowing and "Fordson Majors", and the ever popular David Brown "Cropmasters" which were more suited to baling and collection from the fields. About the time Peter Fitton took these pictures in 1962, I was earning holiday money driving a "Cropmaster", GWR 865 to be exact, and a grand old workhorse she was, very fast in high gears. The smell of freshly baled hay mixed with the scent of warm oil and steam wafting into the carriage is again something one never quite forgets.

(left) 75045 approaches Peel cutting on the 12th August 1962 with a service from Liverpool Exchange. *Peter Fitton*

Up on the roof. 28th September 1964. Peter Fitton joined Frank Dean on the roof of the Electrical works in order to record this busy scene at Spen Dyke. In the foreground, **84016** stands on the loop with **42558.** Meanwhile, the heavy Gresley coaches that make up the "T.V." train are being propelled towards the station by **42625,** which was just passing Rigby Road M.P.D. *Peter Fitton*

76052 station pilot, 12th July 1962. Ex Horwich works and working on trials from Bolton, Neasden's little BR 4 no. **76052** spent a number of days at Blackpool in what was to be an extended series of trials. As well as working various passenger trains to and from Bolton, it acted as station pilot on the 12th and 13th of July, which was when I saw it at Spen Dyke. *Frank Dean.*

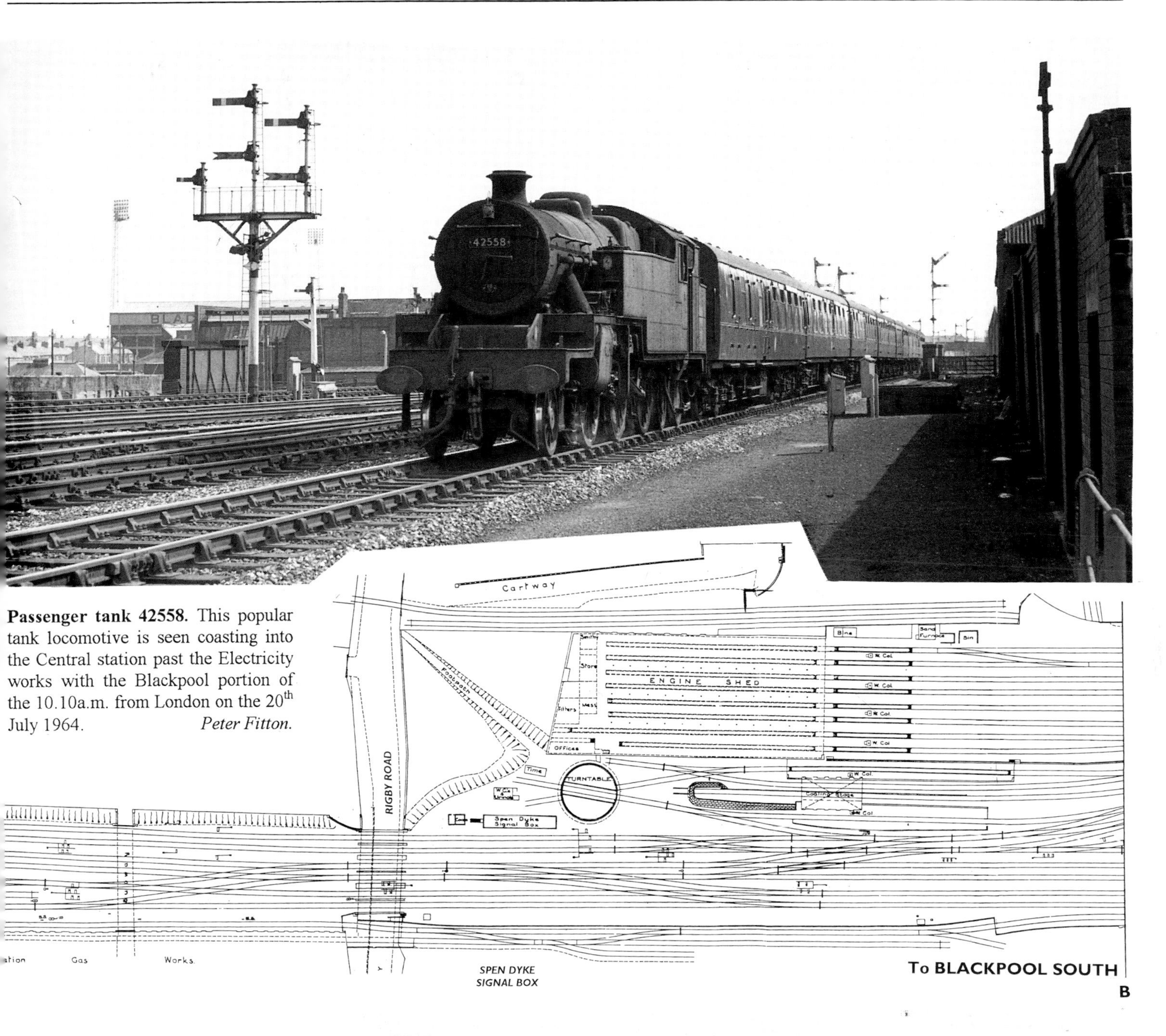

Passenger tank 42558. This popular tank locomotive is seen coasting into the Central station past the Electricity works with the Blackpool portion of the 10.10a.m. from London on the 20th July 1964. *Peter Fitton.*

Spen Dyke signalbox. The large cabin here controlled movements along the main lines as well as the passenger loops and gave access to the motive power depot and the carriage sidings. Working the signalbox here in the summer time was very demanding indeed and the signal men had to be of a very high calibre, such as Archie Buchanan, seen here leaning out of the box window in the summer of 1964. *Archie Buchanan.*

OLD CHARLIE
RUM

From the tower June 1956. What a view! Where do we start....., looking clockwise in the foreground we see the red bricked station frontage complete with red enamel signs and canopy facing onto Bank Hey Street. In the left foreground are the Queens Theatre and Marks and Spencers store at the corner of Albert Road. Central Drive stretches diagonally up the page and on the left are rows of guest houses in roads with names like "Hornby", "Vance" and "Hull", there's even "Coronation Street"... Yes, it was there close by the station running parallel to Central Drive. The excursion concourse is now covered, but not so the platforms numbered 7 to 14. The engine man's lodge house is the building with the "Old Charlie Rum" sign on it, facing Central Drive. Looking along the top of the picture we see the Marton Line climbing away from Blackpool South (right to left) and coming back down the picture the carriage sidings and loco depot are very noticeable as is Bloomfield Road football ground and the Electricity and Gas works at Spen Dyke. Slightly nearer and to the right of the railway is Coop Street where Frank Dean's famous tilting chimney pots could be seen on an out building up to the railway line. Following the railway back down to platforms 1-6, we arrive at the corner of Bonney Street by the New Inn and Station Hotel (bottom right).

British Railways Tourist Department

By the buffers at Blackpool Central

Standing by the buffers. Leaving the platform and making our way out through the barrier at Blackpool Central often left us feeling a little deflated. Sometimes our engine would begin to set back to the carriage sidings at Bloomfield before we had made our way off the platform. "C'mon, lets be having yer", Dad would bellow from the ticket barrier, and with that, off we'd go, heading down the concourse and out onto the streets of Blackpool. Our thoughts however would be firmly fixed upon the events of the last couple of hours. **(above)** By the buffers, we see **42730,** which is on excursion C720 from Bury Knowsley Street, **44893** is on C549 from Radcliffe and the Crab **42924** with the large headboard had come from the Stoke area with a news boys outing. The date is believed to be in June 1961. The little postcard print on the right shows a young Denis Keenan and his mother Norah, who are right in the forefront of the picture. The lady behind with the handbag is Denis's Grandmother, Lizzie Thackrah. They had arrived on the Dewsbury Moor W.M.C. children's trip in June 1952 which had been worked by Low Moor men using Black Five **45208**. Nowadays, a not so young Denis is a train driver at Skipton depot and a good

Pictures of Central. The negative strip seen here was taken by Dave Dyson on a brief trip to Blackpool Central. It includes the print of **42730** on page 96 as well as views of **70048** and **42625** and the station itself. **(Below) 45071** rests by the buffer stops on platform eight, having arrived from Bradford Exchange. Nearer the camera the two old steam heating boilers look in a somewhat weary condition. *Frank Dean.*

sunny

BLACKPOOL

1956

Summer 1956. This aerial view by the British Railways Publicity Dept. is thought to have been taken in the first week of June, at the time of the Raleigh works outing to the resort. It was just a month before our annual trip to Blackpool and some seven weeks before President Nasser took control of the Suez Canal, bringing the threat of yet another war a step nearer. Whilst Dad had been on alert for the Korean War, we were thankful that on this occasion his services would not be required. In the music world, Leeds "loiner" and current "heart-throb", Ronnie Hilton, was topping the pop charts with "No. Other Love", and Hull's David Whitfield, the nations favourite "crooner" had recently released the haunting "My September Love", which stayed in the charts for some 22 weeks. In the 1950's, he rarely seemed to be away from Blackpool during those summer seasons, attracting a huge following wherever he sang. Over a decade had past since the Second World War had ended, yet Britain only just seemed to be waking from its austere post war slumber. Rationing was still fresh in the memory, especially on such things as children's sweets.The railways were still the mainstay in the nation's transport system that would bring the hundreds of thousands of visitors to the resort. Travelling briefly clockwise around the picture, we see in the foreground the cone shaped dome on the corner of the Palatine Hotel. Down on the promenade at this point you can see "O'Hagan's Tea Bar" in the open paved area by the Central Hotel. To the bottom left is the Central station frontage the main yard gates and the little alley leading to Bonney Street. It was this area that became part of the 1959 clearance scheme which would see the demolition of housing and shops close by the station. Up near the top left of the picture, Lytham Road is visible stretching out towards the South. The Pleasure Beach and South Pier guide us back down the picture; the keen eyed amongst you will spot the Manchester Hotel at the corner of Lytham Road. Meanwhile, on the Central Pier, "Jimmy Jewel" minus Ben Warriss is starring with Ken Dodd, Jimmy Clitheroe and young blonde starlet Corinne Grey (see page 95). Between the Central Pier and the corner of Bank Hey Street, the promenade was full of tea bars, cafes, amusements and gypsy fortune tellers. Whilst the Piers are still with us most of the side shows are just like the Central station-merely a fading memory. *Picture by British Railways Publicity Dept; Loaned by Blackpool Corporation Tourist Dept.*

Next.... PART FOUR OF THIS SERIES

RETURN *from* BLACKPOOL CENTRAL

And fare thee weel my only love
And fare thee weel a while
And I will come again my love
Tho' it were 10 thousand mile!

(Above) Departing from Blackpool Central July 1962
(Left) Blackpool - London link driver Bill (Rabbie) Burns
Pictures by G.H.Platt and Don Rutter

ON WE GO WITH PART FOUR OF OUR EXCURSION SERIES. JOIN US AS WE VISIT THE ENGINE SHEDS AT BLACKPOOL'S RIGBY ROAD. SEE THE MOTIVE POWER DOWN ON THE SIDINGS BY BLOOMFIELD TURNTABLE AND AS THE DAYTRIPPERS HEAD HOME AND THE EXCURSION TRAINS LEAVE BLACKPOOL CENTRAL NOSE TO TAIL, TRAVEL HOME WITH US TO EAST LANCASHIRE VIA THE " COAST LINE " (ST. ANNES) ETC., AS WELL AS A DETAILED LOOK AT THE LINE AROUND THE COAST WE'LL BE CALLING AT PRESTON, BLACKBURN, ACCRINGTON, PADIHAM TO ROSE GROVE AND ALL STATIONS TO COLNE. DON'T MISS IT ....ORDER YOUR COPY NOW...!

Travel

THE COAST LINE

ST. ANNES
Ansdell and Fairhaven
LYTHAM